ReadyGEN

Text Collection

GRADE 2

W9-BNQ-716

PEARSON

Glenview, Illinois • Boston, Massachusetts • Chandler, Arizona • Hoboken, New Jersey

Cover: Dean MacAdam

ISBN-13: 978-0-328-85279-6
ISBN-10: 0-328-85279-1
7   19

Table of Contents

Unit 6 Changing the World

Acknowledgments **192**

Seek the Sun

by Phillis Gershator

THE OLD SANDALMAKER and his wife lived in a little wooden house on a sunny street in Asakusa, Japan. For fifty years, husband and wife prayed at the great temple nearby. After they prayed, they chose a paper fortune. Before tying it to a tree, alongside the other paper fortunes fluttering in the breeze, they studied it awhile. Was it a good fortune or a bad one? Sometimes it was hard to tell.

One week their fortune announced: *You will find a way.*

"Yes, I suppose we will," said the sandalmaker.

The next week their fortune advised: *Seek the sun each day.*

"That will be easy," said his wife. "It's springtime, and in the spring, the sun always shines."

But that spring, in the year 1966, a builder came to measure the empty lot across the street. He was followed by three machines and a truckload of men. The men and machines dug a square hole in the ground and drove pilings deep down into the earth. They built walls high up into the sky—one hundred and fifty-four feet high! The new building towered above all the other buildings on the block.

Now the sandalmaker's small two-story house stood in the shade of a nine-story building. When the sandalmaker and his wife rolled up the bed quilts in the morning, even on a sunny morning, it was still dark and cold in their house.

Next door, on the left, the tatami maker's house stood in the shade of the same tall building. The tofu maker's house, on the right, stood in shade, too. The building cast such a long shadow, it kept the sun from shining on all the houses in one whole corner of Asakusa.

The sandalmaker tended to his plants as lovingly as he always had, but his holly tree grew weak in the shade. His tiny bonsai trees stopped bearing fruit.

The breezes that once blew gently in Asakusa now whipped around the tall building. The breezes turned into gusts of wind that lifted the sandalmaker's wife's skirts when she went outside. The wind tore up her umbrella when it rained. The wind grew so fierce, it spun the dust and dirt into swirling tornadoes— and it even uprooted the sandalmaker's precious plants.

"You would think a dragon had moved into the neighborhood!" he cried. "How can we wrestle with a dragon? How can we seek the sun each day here in the shadow of a tall building?"

"We will find a way," said his wife. "Our fortune said so. We will find a way to seek the sun, and our neighbors will help us. We will go to the courthouse and talk to the judge!"

"Our house is cold all the time," the sandalmaker's wife told the judge. "The clothes don't dry. The bed

quilts smell musty. The tatami mats are gathering mold."

"My sandal shop is dark," said the sandalmaker. "I cannot see well enough to work."

"The straw for my mats cannot dry and stretch," said the tatami maker.

"The wind blowing around the tall building blows my cart away," said the tofu maker.

After the judge listened to the townspeople, he listened to the owner of the building.

"We do not have enough land, yet we need more space for offices," explained the builder. "We have no place to build on the ground so we must build up into the sky."

"Yes, that is true," said the judge. "When a city prospers, it does need more space to grow. But it is also true that people live in this city."

And he asked the builder one question: "Would you like to live in a house without sunlight?"

The owner of the tall building bowed his head. "No," he said.

"Sunshine," declared the judge, "is essential to a comfortable life. A citizen's right to enjoy the sunshine in his own home must be protected by law."

The judge ordered the builder to pay the sandalmaker and his neighbors for taking away their sunshine. The judge also ruled that builders could never again build buildings tall enough to block the sun in the narrow streets of Asakusa.

The next time the sandalmaker and his wife visited the great temple, they offered a prayer and chose a paper fortune. The sandalmaker read their fortune out loud. "This one says: *Light will fill an empty space.*"

"It sounds like a good fortune," his wife said, tying it to the branch of a cherry tree. "I hope it comes true."

When the couple arrived home, the only light to fill their house was lantern light. Yet they were happy in the house where they had lived and worked for fifty years, next door to the shops, the temple they loved, and all their good friends. They were happy knowing they had helped to change the laws. "From now on, in neighborhoods like ours," the sandalmaker proudly told his friends, "buildings taller than thirty-three feet will not be allowed."

One sunny morning, after the old couple visited the temple and watched the birds and tourists coming and going, they saw machines and a truckload of men working in an empty lot nearby. The men and machines were digging a hole.

"Oh no! Not another tall building!" cried the

sandalmaker's wife. "How can that be?"

"They are digging a very small hole," observed the sandalmaker.

The next day the hole was filled with water, and the men returned to plant trees, build benches, and lay stone paths. The empty lot had become a park!

"Light will fill an empty space," the sandalmaker

exclaimed. "Our fortune has come true!"

In the park, the sandalmaker's bonsai and holly trees found a new home, and he and his wife found a home away from home: a light-filled space where the bonsai once again bore fruit, schoolchildren and frogs hopped among the stones, and colorful koi swam to and fro in the pond—red, white, and gold beneath the noonday sun.

This story was inspired by an actual court case in Japan, brought by an eighty-year-old sandalmaker, Koji Watanabe, and three of his neighbors in Asakusa, an area in Tokyo known for its famous Buddhist temple and traditional old-style neighborhoods.

Today in Japan, when tall buildings are constructed, the amount of shadow that can fall on nearby buildings is limited by law. In new homes, the law requires that sunlight shine in a family's living room for a certain number of hours each day.

DANGER! EARTHQUAKES

by Seymour Simon

The ground beneath your feet
may seem solid.
But earthquakes make the
ground shake and roll.

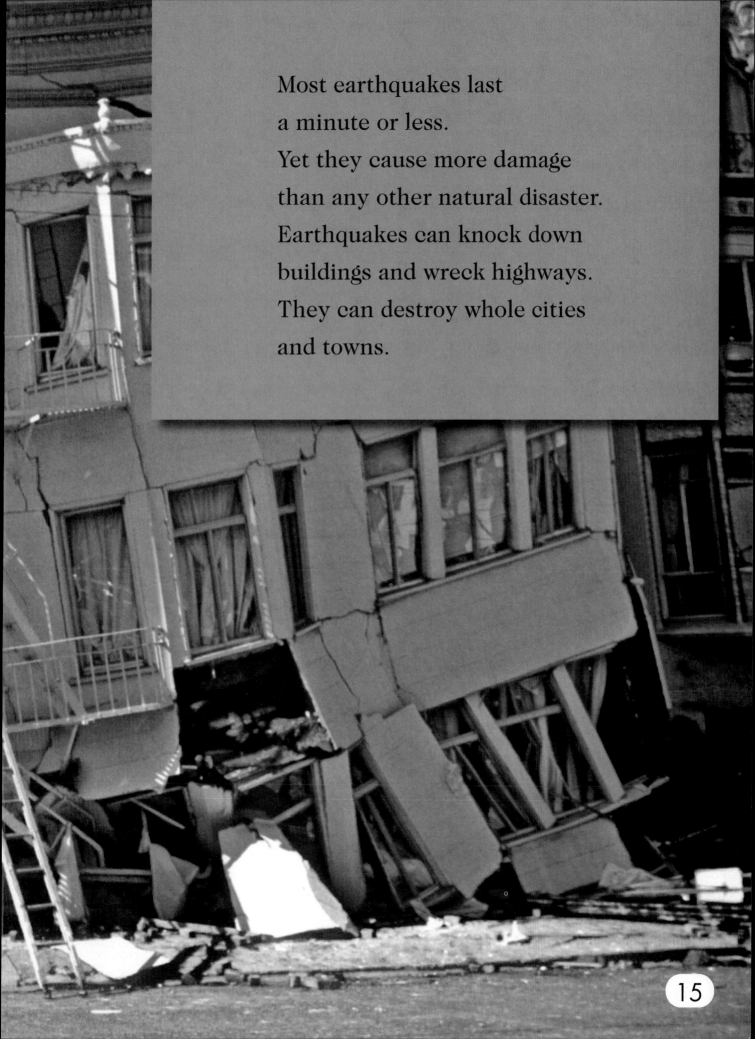

Most earthquakes last
a minute or less.
Yet they cause more damage
than any other natural disaster.
Earthquakes can knock down
buildings and wreck highways.
They can destroy whole cities
and towns.

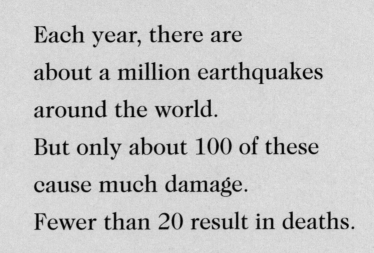

Each year, there are
about a million earthquakes
around the world.
But only about 100 of these
cause much damage.
Fewer than 20 result in deaths.

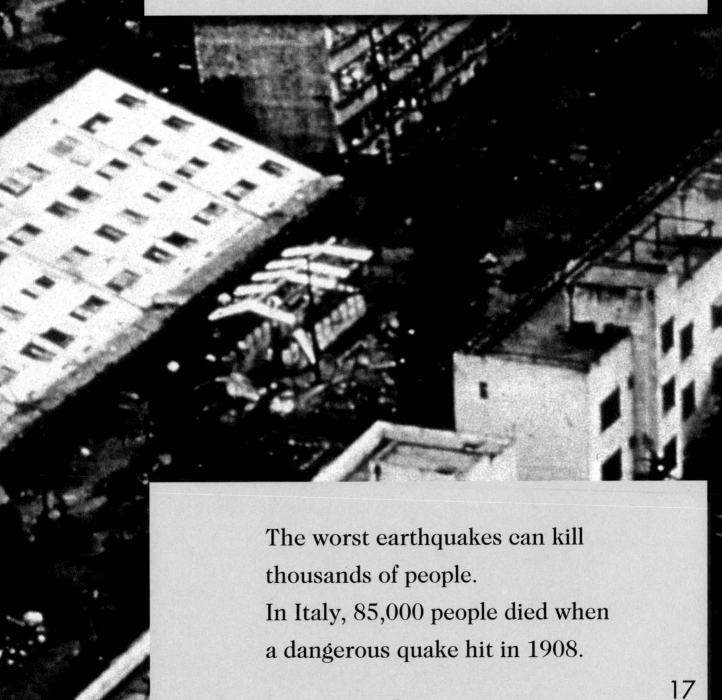

The worst earthquakes can kill
thousands of people.
In Italy, 85,000 people died when
a dangerous quake hit in 1908.

Scientists use the Richter scale
to measure an earthquake's
power.
You may not even notice
a magnitude 2 quake.

You would feel the ground shake
in a magnitude 3 quake.
A magnitude 7 or higher
can destroy a city.
The largest recorded earthquake
was a 9.5 in Chile in 1960.

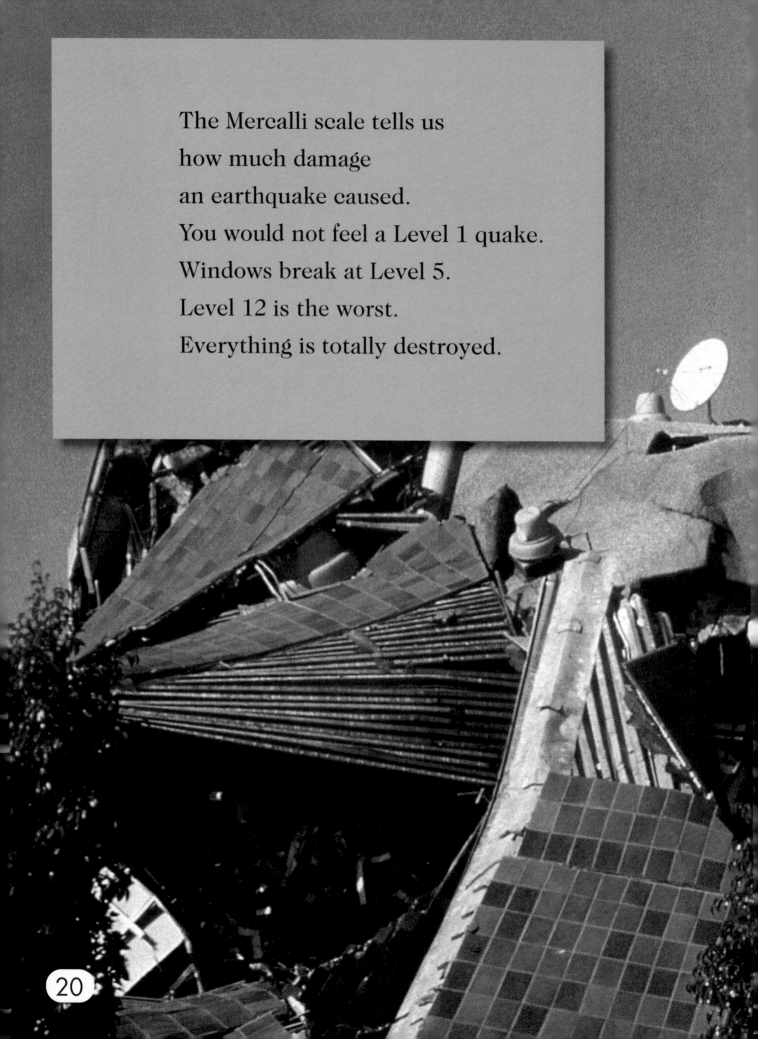

The Mercalli scale tells us
how much damage
an earthquake caused.
You would not feel a Level 1 quake.
Windows break at Level 5.
Level 12 is the worst.
Everything is totally destroyed.

The earthquake that shook
San Francisco in October 1989
measured 7.1 on the Richter scale.
On the Mercalli scale,
it measured from 6 to 11
in different parts of the city.

Most of the world's earthquakes
happen in a zone called the
Pacific Ring of Fire.

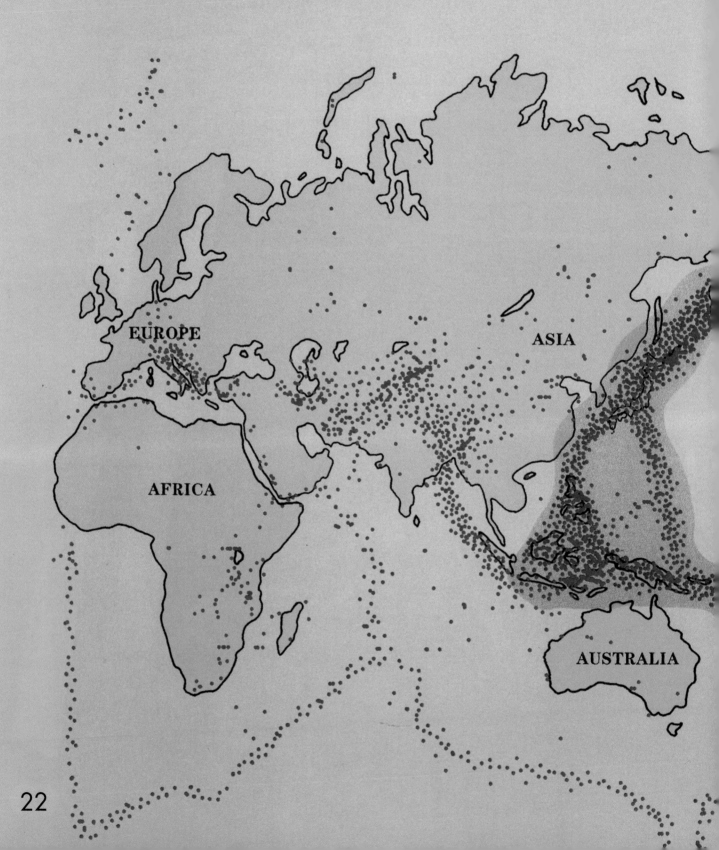

EUROPE

ASIA

AFRICA

AUSTRALIA

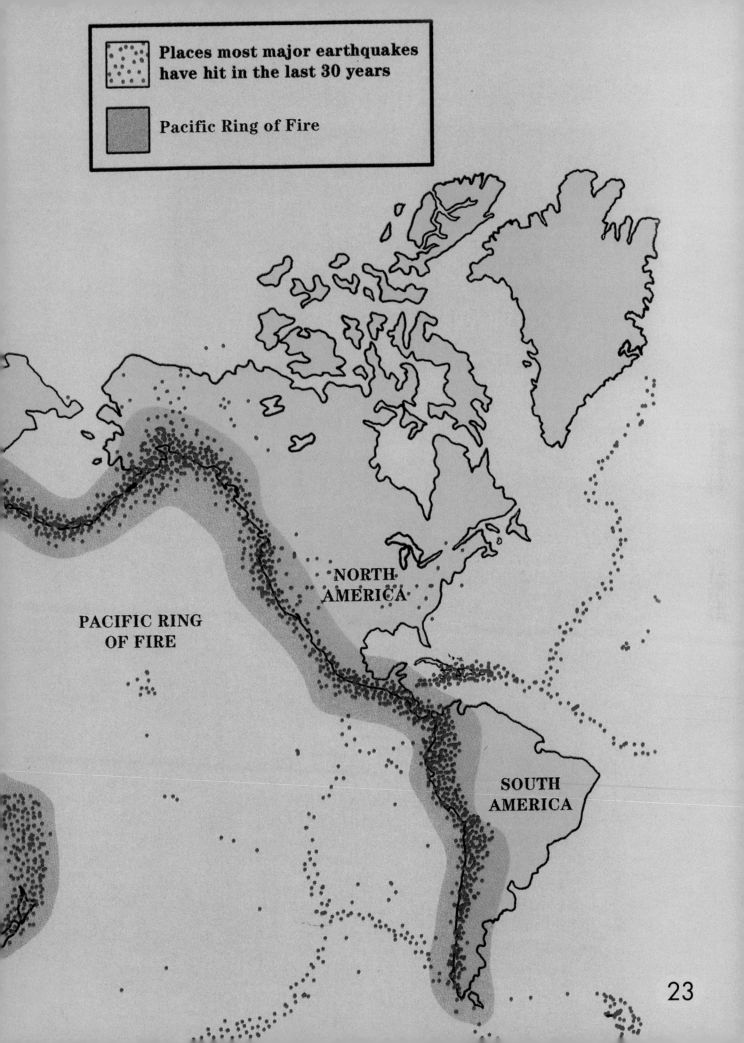

Places most major earthquakes
have hit in the last 30 years

Pacific Ring of Fire

PACIFIC RING
OF FIRE

NORTH
AMERICA

SOUTH
AMERICA

23

Most earthquakes begin
in the earth's crust.
The crust is a layer of rocks
that covers the earth.
It is 5 to 30 miles deep.
Cracks in the rocks run
through the crust.

These are called fault zones.
The rocks on one side
of a crack push against
the rocks on the other side.
The rocks may stay in place for
years, but then they suddenly
slide past each other.

What makes the rocks move?
The answer lies below the crust,
in the mantle.
The mantle is a 2,000-mile-thick
layer of melted rock.
Over millions of years,
movements in the mantle have
cracked the crust into huge
floating pieces called plates.

These plates grind
past each other
at about two inches per year.
That's about as fast as
your fingernails grow.
The layers of rock in this photo
folded because of
movements in the mantle.

The San Andreas fault lies
between the North American
and the Pacific plates.
It runs for 700 miles through
Southern California to just north
of San Francisco.

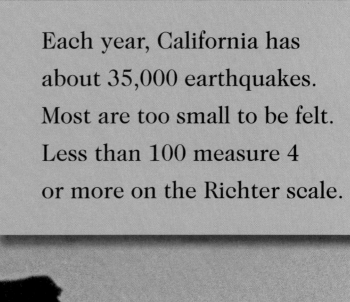

Each year, California has
about 35,000 earthquakes.
Most are too small to be felt.
Less than 100 measure 4
or more on the Richter scale.

Alaska has more earthquakes
than any other state.
Alaska has a magnitude 7 quake
almost every year.
Earthquakes also occur
in the central United States.
In 1811, an 8+ quake shook
the Mississippi valley.
It caused church bells to ring in
Boston, nearly 1,000 miles away.

31

The most violent earthquake
ever recorded in the United
States took place in Anchorage,
Alaska, in March 1964.
The quake measured 8.4
on the Richter scale
and 10 on the Mercalli scale.
Cracks in the earth up to 30 feet
wide opened like giant jaws.
Nearby ports were completely
destroyed by huge sea waves.
More than 100 people died.

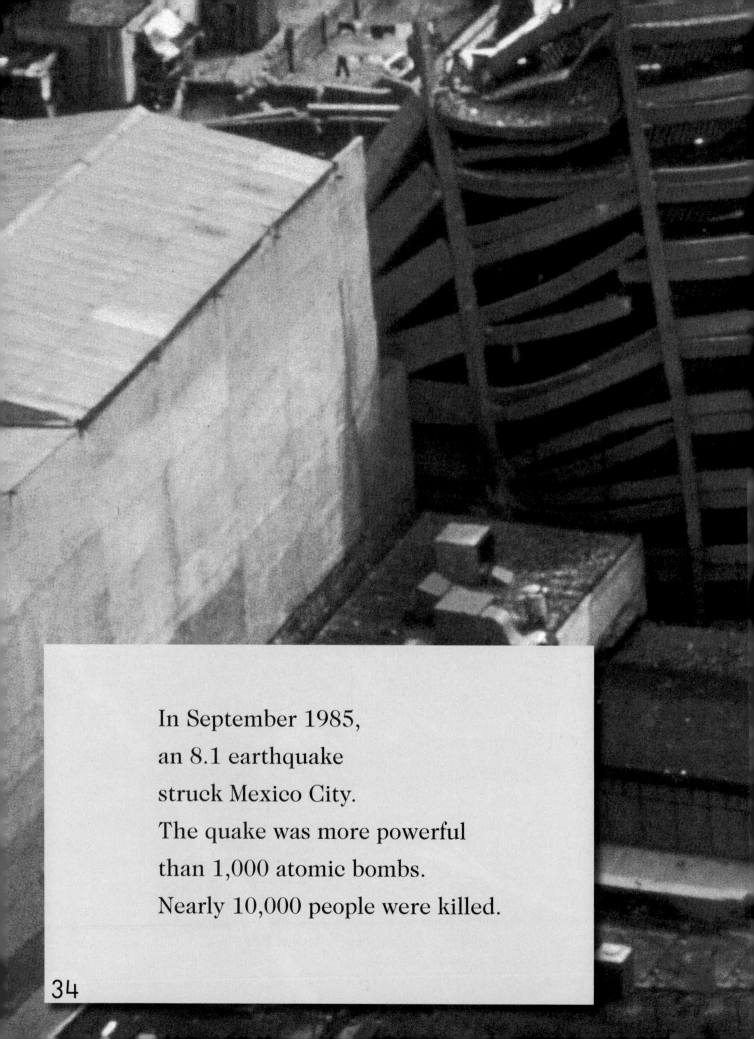

In September 1985,
an 8.1 earthquake
struck Mexico City.
The quake was more powerful
than 1,000 atomic bombs.
Nearly 10,000 people were killed.

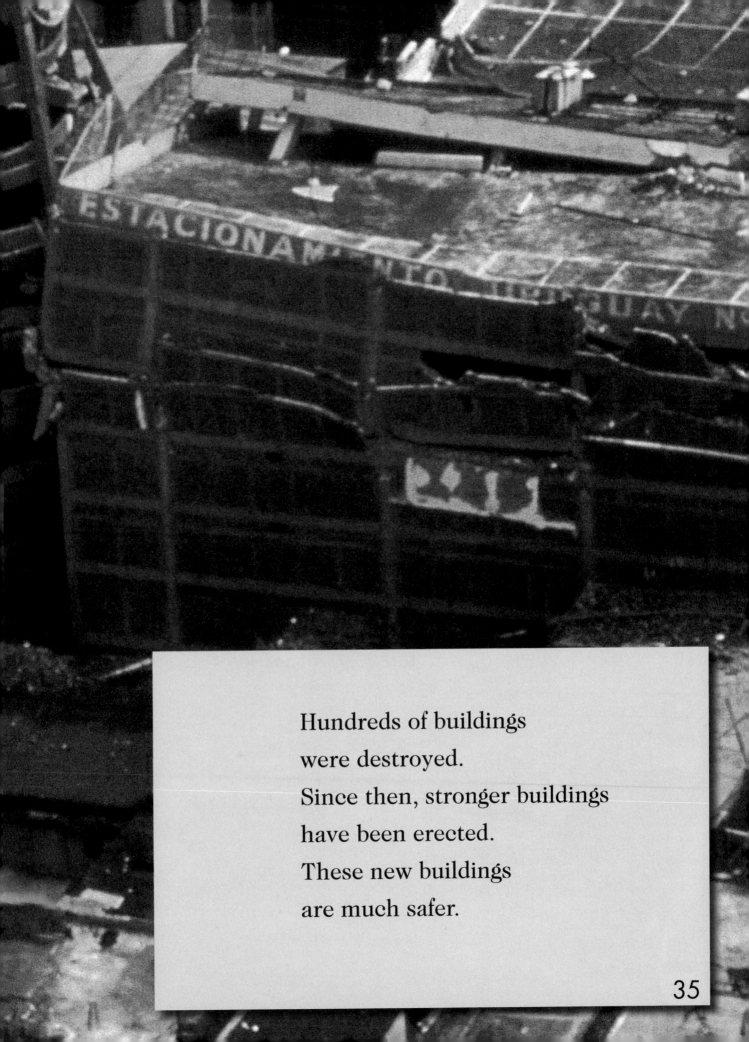

Hundreds of buildings
were destroyed.
Since then, stronger buildings
have been erected.
These new buildings
are much safer.

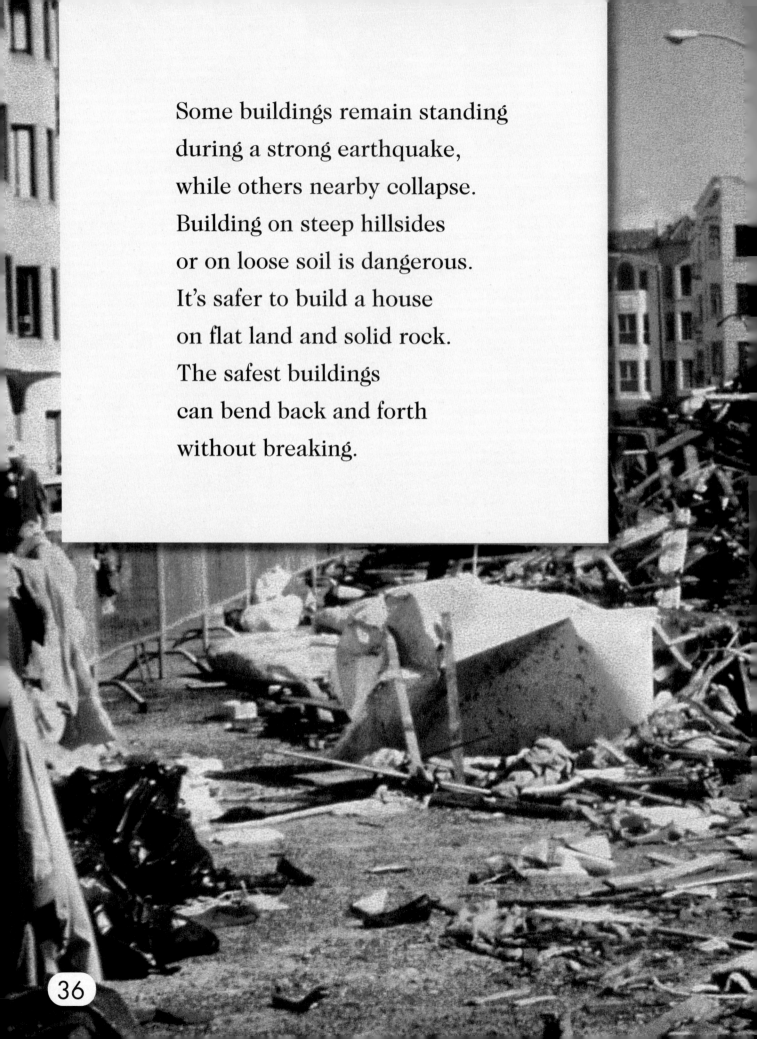

Some buildings remain standing
during a strong earthquake,
while others nearby collapse.
Building on steep hillsides
or on loose soil is dangerous.
It's safer to build a house
on flat land and solid rock.
The safest buildings
can bend back and forth
without breaking.

Scientists use machines
that can measure and record
earthquake activity.
They can also tell us where
earthquakes are likely to strike.

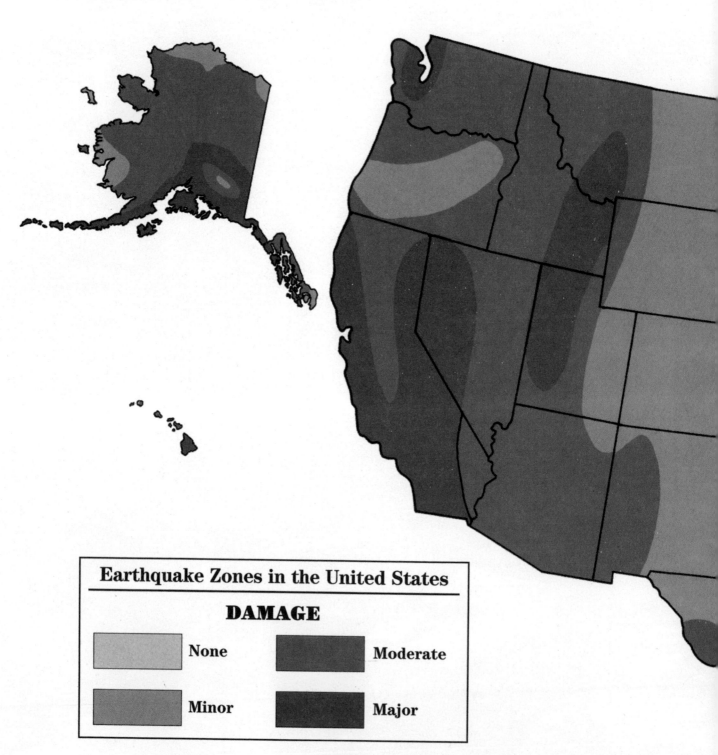

Earthquake Zones in the United States

DAMAGE

None

Moderate

Minor

Major

But they cannot yet tell us
exactly when, where, or how big
an earthquake will be.

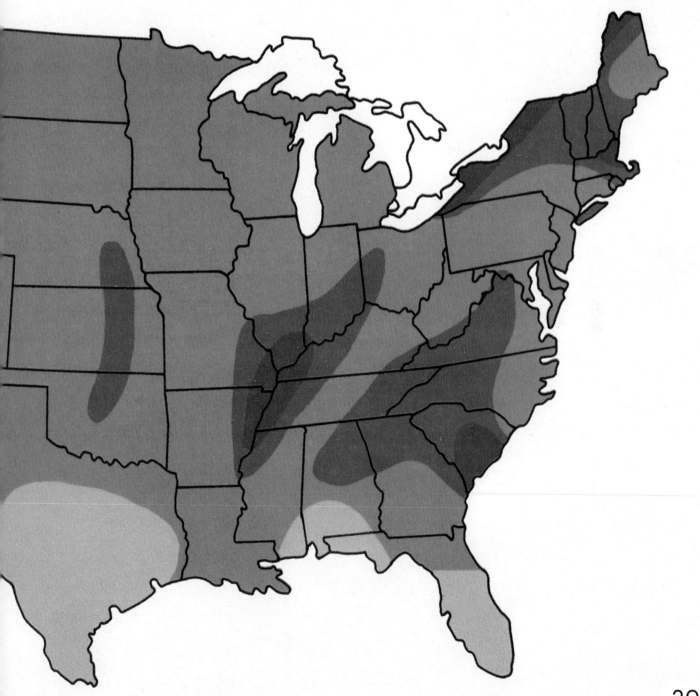

Here is what to do
if you are in an earthquake.
If you are indoors, stay there.
Take cover under a sturdy table,
desk, or bed.
Stay away from windows,
mirrors, and high cabinets.
If you are outdoors,
move away from power lines
and tall buildings.

No one can prevent earthquakes.
But in the future we will be able
to reduce the damage they cause.

The Fool on the Hill
from Harry Devlin's "Tales of Thunder and Lightning"

A Russian Tale

Once upon a time, in a great castle atop a steep hill, there lived a wizard and his beautiful daughter. At the foot of the same hill, in a sad and sorry hovel, the village fool made his home.

Somehow, the fool had gotten it into his head that the lovely maiden was being held captive by a wicked sorcerer. So, from time to time, he would decide to rescue her. Arming himself with a homemade wooden lance and shield, and protecting his head with a copper tea kettle, the fool stormed the castle hill in order to save the fair damsel.

The wizard, of course, always heard the fool climbing clumsily upward. And from his bag of tricks he would draw forth magical balls of fire — lightning — to frighten away the poor simpleton. As the surprised fool toppled noisily back down the hill — head (and tea kettle) over heels — the beautiful maid would join her father in loud hoots of laughter.

All this noise is what makes Russian thunder!

Mother of the Mountains

from Harry Devlin's "Tales of Thunder and Lightning"

An American Indian Legend

The Catskill Mountain region of New York is justly famous for its magnificent storms. The sounds of thunder echo and re-echo across its great Hudson River and valleys.

The Indians who lived here before the white man came believed that an old and wise spirit, the Mother of the Mountains, made her home on the Catskills' highest peak. And, so long as she felt pleased with her people in the valleys below, she would spin light summery clouds out of cobwebs and morning dew.

But whenever she was annoyed, the Mother of the Mountains would take out her big cooking cauldron and stir up a batch of heavy storm clouds. Black as ink and alive with the fire of her anger, these weighty clouds soon burst over the valleys, making thunderous booms and releasing bolts of fiery lightning.

A drenching rain usually followed.

45

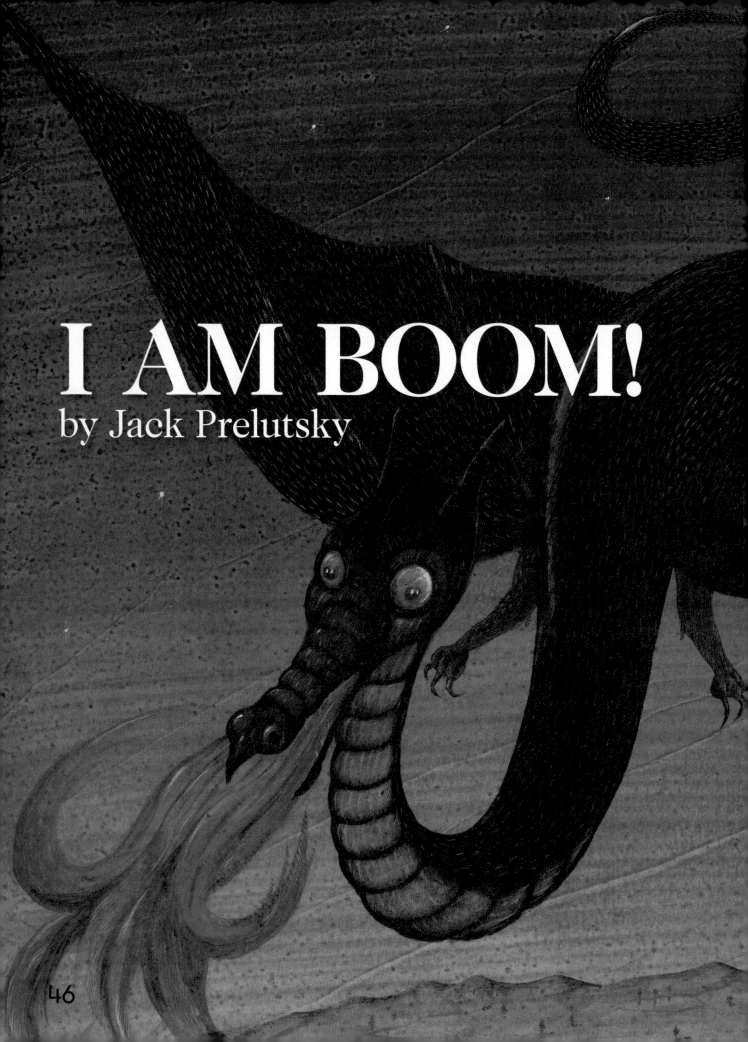

I AM BOOM!
by Jack Prelutsky

I am Boom the thunder dragon,
Taller than the tallest trees,
I stir whirlwinds when I whisper,
Mighty cyclones when I sneeze,
Fishes shiver in the ocean
When I tread upon the shore,
I make earthquakes and volcanoes
When I roar roar **roar!**

I am Boom the thunder dragon,
All the earth is my domain,
When I flap my wings in fury,
I create a hurricane,
Lions vanish at my footsteps,
Eagles tremble at my glance,
And the mountains start to rumble
When I dance dance **dance!**

Giants fly into a panic
When I rear my massive head,
When I snort my searing fires,
Fearless ogres faint with dread,
If you ever see me coming,
You had better give me room,
I am Boom the thunder dragon,
I am BOOM! BOOM! **BOOM!**

Dragon Smoke

by Lilian Moore

Breathe and blow
white clouds
    with every puff.
It's cold today,
    cold enough
to see your breath.
Huff!
    Breathe dragon smoke
      today!

Who Could Somersault the San Andreas Fault?

by J. Patrick Lewis

No one could possibly pole-vault
Or trampoline or somersault
Across the San Andreas fault.

The one unlucky lad who tried—
From Malibu to Riverside—
Could feel the continent divide!

600 miles long and 20 deep—
Now that is something of a leap.
I think *I'll* stay in bed and sleep.

Anyway, the
road signs
warn ya:

NO JUMPING
OVER
CALIFORNIA!

Johnny Appleseed

by Lola M. Schaefer

First Biographies

Time Line

1774
born

John Chapman was born
in Massachusetts in 1774.
John liked to walk and
play in the woods.

◀ Massachusetts woods

Time Line

1774
born

around 1794
travels west

John wanted to see
the frontier and help the
settlers. Around 1794,
John left his home. He
started walking west.

Time Line

1774
born

around 1794
travels west

1797
settles in
Pennsylvania

In 1797, John settled in Pennsylvania. He collected apple seeds from nearby cider mills.

pressing apples to make cider, 1800s

Time Line

1774
born

around 1794
travels west

1797
settles in
Pennsylvania

John knew that apples were
a good food that would last
through the long winter.
He planted the apple seeds.
Apple trees began to grow
on his land.

Time Line

1774
born

around 1794
travels west

1797
settles in
Pennsylvania

John dug up some of
the young apple trees.
He planted new orchards
with them.

Time Line

1774
born

around 1794
travels west

1797
settles in
Pennsylvania

In the early 1800s,
John moved west again.
He moved to Ohio. He
sold or gave apple
seeds and trees to
many settlers there.

picking apples, 1800s

early 1800s
moves to Ohio

Time Line

1774
born

around 1794
travels west

1797
settles in
Pennsylvania

John liked to read books.
Sometimes he read to
the settlers. Other times
he told stories about
himself and his apples.

Johnny Appleseed (on floor) reading to settlers

early 1800s
moves to Ohio

Time Line

1774
born

around 1794
travels west

1797
settles in
Pennsylvania

In 1838, John moved
to Indiana. He sold
apple seeds and trees
to the settlers. He helped
the settlers plant orchards.

Johnny Appleseed planting an orchard

early 1800s
moves to Ohio

1838
moves to Indiana

Time Line

1774
born

around 1794
travels west

1797
settles in
Pennsylvania

John shared apple seeds,
apple trees, and stories.
Settlers gave him the
nickname Johnny Appleseed.
He died in Indiana
in 1845.

◀ Johnny Appleseed's gravesite

early 1800s
moves to Ohio

1838
moves to Indiana

1845
dies

GOING WEST

by Jean Van Leeuwen

pictures by Thomas B. Allen

One day in early spring we packed everything
we had into our wagon, tied our milk cow Sadie
on behind, and set out to find a new home.
 Going West.

There were five of us: Papa and Mama;
me, Hannah, just turned seven; my little
brother Jake; and Rebecca, a fat baby with
yellow curls.

74

Mama cried. She was leaving her three
sisters and all our furniture and the piano she
loved to play. But Papa said we were going
to a place where anything you planted would
grow and a farm could stretch out as far
as the eye could see.

We left behind the town we knew, the woods,
the hills. We rode, bouncing and swaying in
the creaking wagon, day after day.

At night Mama cooked over a campfire
and we slept close together on the wagon floor,
with stars winking through the opening in
our canvas roof.

Here is what was in our wagon: blankets and pillows and quilts, Mama's favorite rocking chair, trunks full of clothes, barrels full of food, a cookstove, a box of tin dishes, all of Mama's cooking pots, all of Papa's tools, a Bible, a rifle, and a spinning wheel.

There was barely room for us.

Sometimes it rained. Our wagon got stuck in the mud and we all had to get out and push. Once it rained so hard that the wagon leaked. That night we slept in wet clothes in wet beds, without any supper. Rebecca cried, and Jake said he wanted to go home. Mama didn't say anything, but I think she felt the same.

We were all tired of the rocking wagon and the dust and the same sights day after day. Jake fell out and hurt his arm. Rebecca caught a cold. At night she coughed and coughed. Mama looked worried, but still we rode on.

Going West.

We came to a river, all muddy and wide.

"How will we get across?" I asked Papa.

"The horses will take us," he said.

First the water came up to the horses' knees.

And then their chests.

Suddenly Papa shouted, "Hold on tight!"
The horses were swimming. Water was pouring
into the wagon. Mama held me tight, until at last
I felt the horses' feet touch bottom again.
We had crossed the river.

On the other side of the river the land was flat, with no trees. There was not a bush and not a stone; nothing but green, waving grass and blue sky and a constant, whispering wind. It seemed a lonely, empty place.

But Papa said, "This is the land we've been looking for."

As the sun was setting, we came upon a place where wildflowers bloomed in mounds of pink and lavender and blue, like soft pillows.

"Look," said Mama, smiling.

And Papa said, "Here is where we will build our house."

The next day we began. Papa took the
horses and rode away. When he came back,
he brought logs from the creek. For many days
he worked. Slowly, with Mama helping, he
built walls, a roof, a door.

Finally he took Mama's rocking chair and set it next to our new fireplace. It was only one room, with dirt for a floor; but at last we slept in a house again.

Mama planted a garden. Jake carried water from the creek to do the washing. I minded the baby and swept the dirt floor and helped Mama hang checked curtains on the window.

"There," she said. "We are ready for visitors."

But no visitors came. We were alone on the vast prairie.

Papa rode away again, many miles to town.
For three long days we watched and waited.
And then Papa came back. He brought flour
and bacon and six sheep that he traded for one
of the horses and a surprise: real white sugar.

Mama baked a cake and it reminded me
of home.

Summer came. A hot wind blew.
Papa went out hunting for rabbits, and
Jake and I picked blackberries next to
the creek.

Mama lay down in the grass with the sheep.

"Oh my," she sighed when we found her. "This is a lonesome land."

Day after day the sun beat down, baking our little house, shriveling up the plants in the garden. It was so hot that nothing moved, not even the wind.

"If only we had a tree for shade," said Mama.

One afternoon when Jake and I were at the creek, dark clouds suddenly covered the sun. Thunder rumbled and lightning flashed. We ran for home. But before we got there, hail came tumbling out of the sky, big and round and hard as marbles.

"Quick!" I shouted. "The buckets!" We put them over our heads and kept running.

Mama was waiting at the door. "Thank goodness you're safe," she said.

When the storm was over, Mama's garden was squashed flat. "The land is good," she said. "But the weather is hard."

"Never mind," said Papa. "In the spring we will plant again."

Mama was frying donuts and Jake and I were doing our lessons on the dirt floor, when visitors finally came: Indians! Jake hid under the bed. I crept behind the rocking chair, my knees trembling with fright. They looked so fierce.

But Mama smiled. She gave one of the Indians a donut. The Indian smiled. Mama kept on making donuts and the Indians kept on eating donuts until Papa came home. And then the Indians went away.

The wind turned cold. Mama stored up potatoes and berries and nuts for the long winter to come. Papa went hunting for deer. He came back with Mr. Swenson. Mr. Swenson stayed for supper and afterward he played his flute while Mama sang, sitting around the fire. And suddenly the prairie wasn't empty anymore.

We had a neighbor.

"Do they have Christmas out here?"
Jake asked. And I wondered too.

But Mama said, "Of course."

So we hung our stockings by the chimney.
Rebecca got a cup and Jake a whistle and I
found Nelly, a rag doll with yellow braids.
Later we had wild turkey for dinner and
Mama opened the jam she had been saving
all year.

And everything was just like Christmas.

106

Now the icy wind seeped through cracks in our log walls. We put on all the clothes we had and huddled next to the fire. One morning it was so cold that Mama's fresh-baked bread was frozen solid. And then it began to snow.

It snowed for three days and three nights. Papa tied a rope from the house to the stable so he could feed the animals.

Jake and I did our lessons and Mama helped me sew on my quilt and we all listened to the wind howling outside.

At last everything grew still. Looking out, we saw no woodpile, no stable, no sky, nothing but snow drifting up to the roof of our little house.

It was a long, cold winter. We had nothing to eat but potatoes and hard biscuits and nuts. Rebecca cried because she was hungry. And one day Mama counted the potatoes and said, "There are only six left."

But then slowly the snow began to melt. Each day the drifts under our window grew smaller. Papa took down his rifle and went hunting again. And that night the smell of rabbit stew made our house warm once more.

One morning when the grass was turning new green, Papa said, "It's planting time."

He hitched our horse to the plow and broke through the tough prairie grass to the dark, rich soil beneath. For days he worked, plowing long, straight rows. Then Mama dropped in seeds and Jake and I covered them up. The warm sun shone. The seeds sprouted. And all around us, as far as my eyes could see, was our farm.

It was Mama's birthday. Jake and I
picked flowers for the table. Papa brought
home a surprise: a little tree from the creek
to plant by the front door.

"Next year if the corn does well," he
said, "we will buy a piano."

And Mr. Swenson came for dinner with
another surprise: his new wife.

"Welcome to our house," said Mama.
We ate Mama's food and listened to Mrs.
Swenson tell about back East and sang,
sitting around the fire. Outside, a soft wind
was blowing in the new corn.

I looked around at Mama in her rocking chair and
Rebecca sleeping and Jake leaning on Papa's knee.
And our house felt like home.

From...
Planting a Tree
by Nancy Byrd Turner

Firm in the good brown earth
Set we our little tree.
Clear dews will freshen it,
Cool rain will feed it,
Sun will be warming it
As warmth is needed.
Winds will blow round it free—
Take root, good tree!

TREES

by Harry Behn

Trees are the kindest things I know,
They do no harm, they simply grow

And spread a shade for sleepy cows,
And gather birds among their boughs.

They give us fruit in leaves above,
And wood to make our houses of,

And leaves to burn on Hallowe'en,
And in the Spring new buds of green.

They are the first when day's begun
To touch the beams of morning sun,

They are the last to hold the light
When evening changes into night,

And when a moon floats on the sky
They hum a drowsy lullaby

Of sleepy children long ago …
Trees are the kindest things I know.

Home on the Range

by Dr. Brewster Higley

Oh, give me a home where the Buffalo roam
Where the Deer and the Antelope play;
Where seldom is heard a discouraging word,
And the sky is not cloudy all day.

▶**Chorus**

A home! A home!
Where the Deer and the Antelope play,
Where seldom is heard a discouraging word,
And the sky is not cloudy all day.

Oh! give me a land where the bright diamond sand
Throws its light from the glittering streams,
Where glideth along the graceful white swan,
Like the maid in her heavenly dreams.

Chorus

How often at night, when the heavens were bright,
With the light of the twinkling stars
Have I stood here amazed, and asked as I gazed,
If their glory exceed that of ours.

Chorus

I love the wild flowers in this bright land of ours,
I love the wild curlew's shrill scream;
The bluffs and white rocks, and antelope flocks
That graze on the mountains so green.

Chorus

The Gateway Arch
St. Louis, Missouri
by Diane Siebert

It stands, the gateway to the West—
An arch of steel, shining
With sunlight glinting off its crest,
Its silhouette defining

St. Louis and the role it played
In settling a nation—
A crossroads and a place of trade
Amid the great migration

Of settlers traveling, westward bound,
With dreams enough to carry
Them over harsh, unbroken ground
To plain and peak and prairie.

And now, to honor times gone by
And years that lie behind us,
The Gateway Arch, whose steel meets sky
Stands proudly…to remind us.

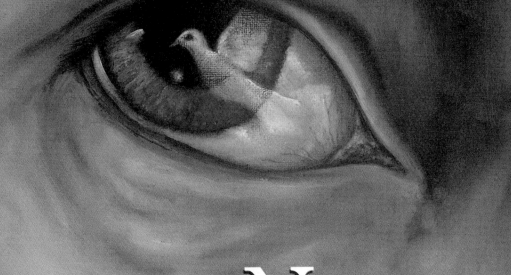

ALFRED NOBEL
THE MAN BEHIND THE PEACE PRIZE

BY KATHY-JO WARGIN

AND ILLUSTRATED BY ZACHARY PULLEN

The hammer dropped with a bang! Upon the anvil was a drop of liquid nitroglycerin.

Startled, Alfred Nobel began to think about the power of the liquid.

A liquid like this could cause enough force to blast away rock where bridges and roads and railways needed to be built. It could help militaries have safer weapons. Most often, gunpowder was used for these purposes, but it wasn't very safe. Alfred's love of poetry and literature was equal to his love of science and chemistry. Although he hoped to spend his life as a writer, he soon realized that writing and poetry would have to wait.

Alfred began trying different ways to ignite nitroglycerin safely. With the help of his father and brothers Robert and Ludvig, he experimented day and night, sometimes mixing the liquid with gunpowder, which made it easier to handle.

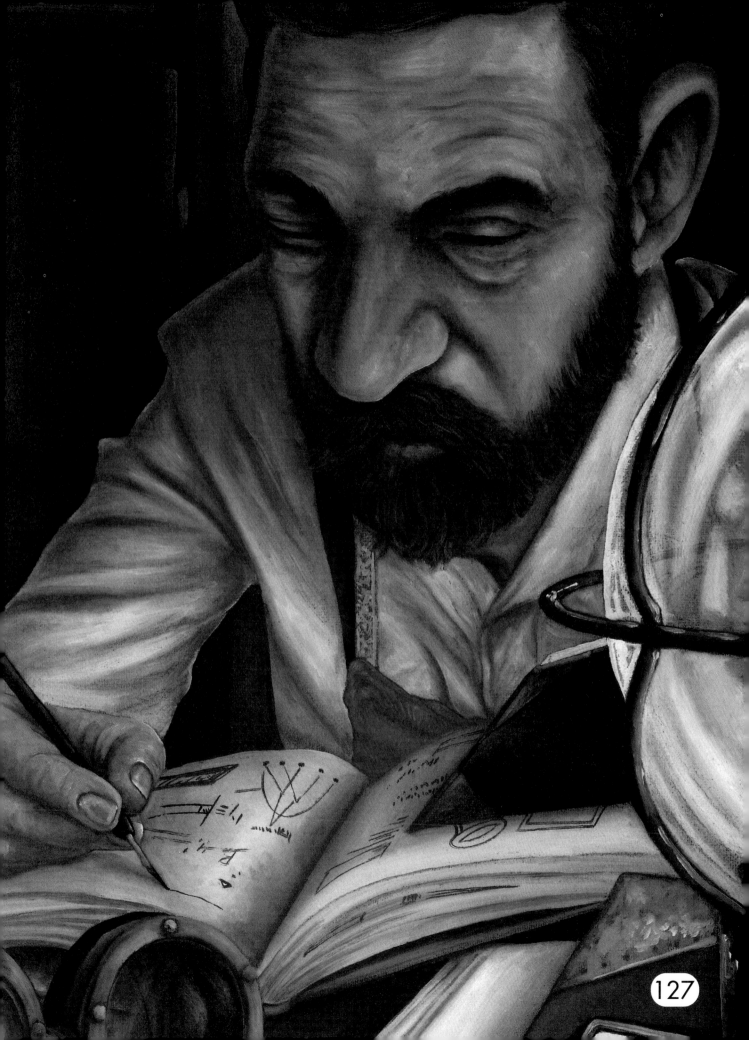

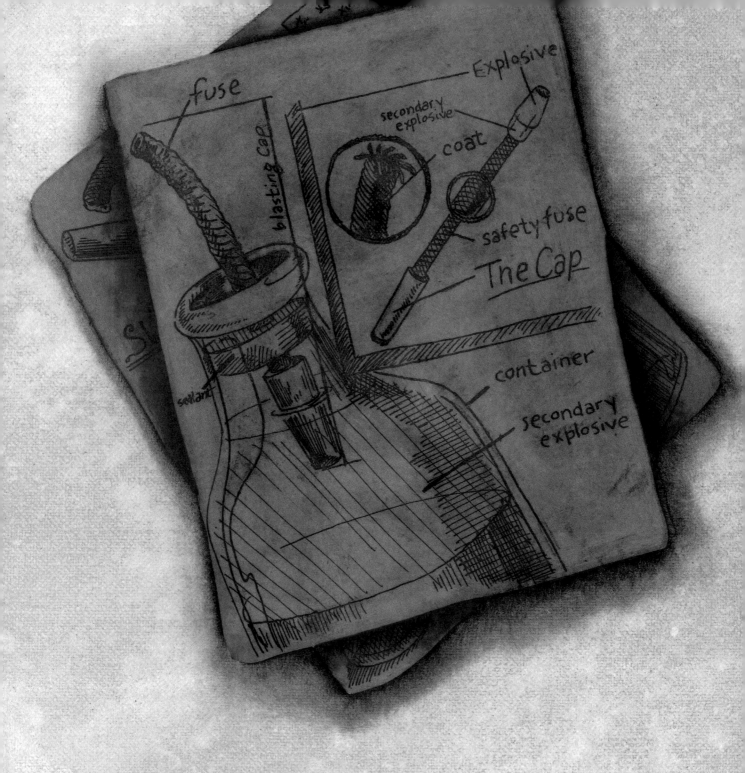

Alfred kept testing until he came up with a wooden plug he could fill with gunpowder. He called the plug a blasting cap. It would help builders ignite the nitroglycerin safely. Alfred was pleased.

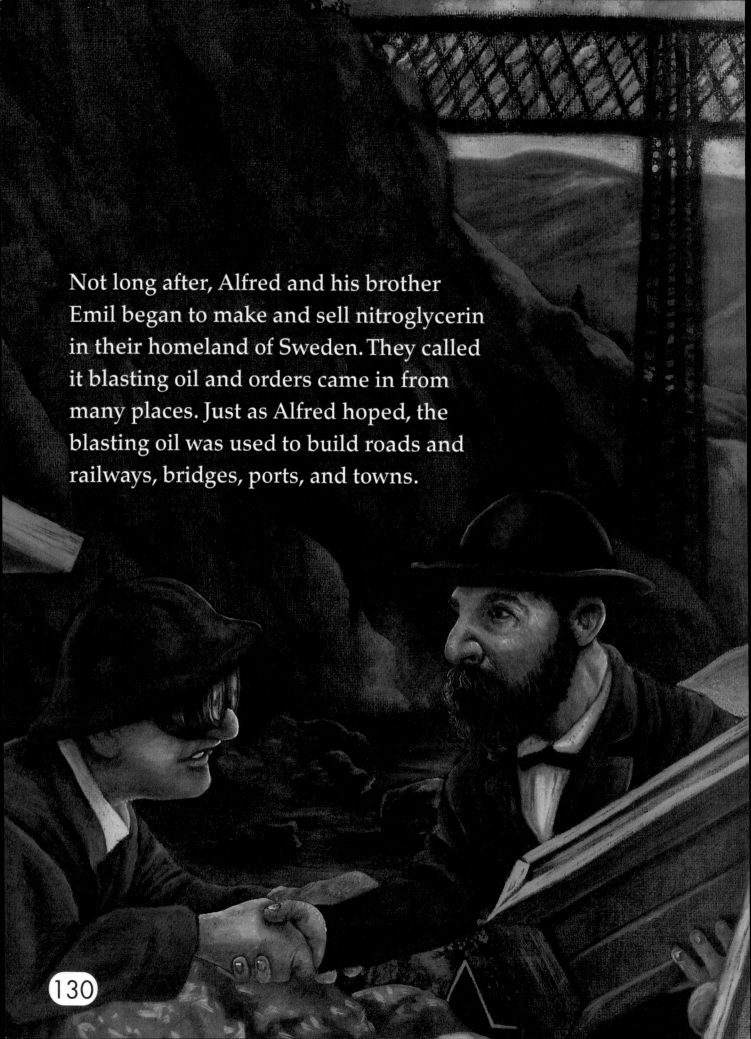

Not long after, Alfred and his brother
Emil began to make and sell nitroglycerin
in their homeland of Sweden. They called
it blasting oil and orders came in from
many places. Just as Alfred hoped, the
blasting oil was used to build roads and
railways, bridges, ports, and towns.

One day in the workshop, Emil and a partner were making some new oil when something went terribly wrong.

BOOM!

Everything exploded, and five people were dead, including Emil.

The tragedy proved one thing to Alfred. He must make nitroglycerin even safer yet. As the pain of his loss troubled him, Alfred worked day and night. Some days he would feel weak and ill, while others he felt lonely and sad, wanting nothing more than to escape into books or poetry.

Two years after Emil died, Alfred mixed nitroglycerin with sand. This made a paste he could roll into the shape of a rod. He realized such rods could be put into holes so builders could make blasts happen only where they wanted. The rods would ignite only if they had a blasting cap, making them unlikely to explode on their own. Finally, Alfred Nobel made nitroglycerin safe to use.

Alfred named his invention after the Greek word *dynamis*, which means power. But to the world, Alfred Nobel had invented something called dynamite.

This made Alfred wealthy and famous. Everybody knew about Alfred Nobel and his dynamite.

Alfred was happy with his success. Most of all, he hoped his inventions would prevent war. He thought that if people were afraid of the harm that explosions could cause, perhaps they would settle things peacefully first.

But Alfred was wrong.

In many countries, people began to use dynamite to solve problems by hurting others. This made Alfred very sad.

One morning in France, where Alfred was living, people woke to the newspaper headline, "Alfred Nobel Is Dead!"' It reported that Alfred Nobel, the dynamite king, had died of a heart attack. People everywhere were shocked by the news, but nobody was more shocked than Alfred Nobel.

His brother Ludvig had recently died. The newspaper had reported it wrong.

As Alfred read his own obituary, he realized that others saw him as a man who earned his wealth by inventing ways to injure and kill. For the rest of his days, this made him very sad.

On December 10, 1896, Alfred Nobel died a wealthy but lonely man at his home in Italy. He was buried in Sweden.

His friends and family gathered to hear the reading of his will. After money had been given to a few close friends and relatives, an announcement was made. The entire estate of Alfred Nobel, one of the richest men in all of Europe, would be used to create yearly prizes for those who have rendered the greatest services to humankind.

There would be a prize for accomplishment in physics; another for chemical discovery or improvement; a prize for physiology or medicine; and a prize for literature.

And last was to be a special prize. It would be for peace.

So on that very day, Alfred Nobel, the man who loved literature and poetry and the art of discovery, left a legacy to be remembered for always—as the man who founded what became known throughout the world as The Nobel Prizes.

THE NOBEL PEACE PRIZE WINNERS

The Nobel Peace Prize has been awarded to individuals or organizations since 1901. For years not listed on the following chart, no prize was awarded. To learn more about Alfred Nobel and the Nobel Prizes, visit Nobelprize.org.

2008 MARTTI AHTISAARI

2007 *Intergovernmental Panel on Climate Change,* AL GORE

2006 MUHAMMAD YUNUS, *Grameen Bank*

2005 *International Atomic Energy Agency,* MOHAMED ELBARADEI

2004 WANGARI MAATHAI

2003 SHIRIN EBADI

2002 JIMMY CARTER

2001 *United Nations,* KOFI ANNAN

2000 KIM DAE-JUNG

1999 MÉDECINS SANS FRONTIÈRES

1998 JOHN HUME, DAVID TRIMBLE

1997 *International Campaign to Ban Landmines,* JODY WILLIAMS

1996 CARLOS FILIPE XIMENES BELO, JOSÉ RAMOS-HORTA

1995 JOSEPH ROTBLAT, *Pugwash Conferences on Science and World Affairs*

1994 YASSER ARAFAT, SHIMON PERES, YITZHAK RABIN

1993 NELSON MANDELA, F.W. DE KLERK

1992 RIGOBERTA MENCHÚ TUM

1991 AUNG SAN SUU KYI

1990 MIKHAIL GORBACHEV

1989 THE 14TH DALAI LAMA

1988 *United Nations Peacekeeping Forces*

1987 OSCAR ARIAS SÁNCHEZ

1986 ELIE WIESEL

1985 *International Physicians for the Prevention of Nuclear War*

1984 DESMOND TUTU

1983 LECH WALESA

1982 ALVA MYRDAL, ALFONSO GARCÍA ROBLES

1981 *Office of the United Nations High Commissioner for Refugees*

1980 ADOLFO PÉREZ ESQUIVEL

1979 MOTHER TERESA

1978 ANWAR AL-SADAT, MENACHEM BEGIN

1977 *Amnesty International*

1976 BETTY WILLIAMS, MAIREAD CORRIGAN

1975 ANDREI SAKHAROV

1974 SEÁN MACBRIDE, EISAKU SATO

1973 HENRY KISSINGER, LE DUC THO

1971 WILLY BRANDT

1970 NORMAN BORLAUG

1969 *International Labour Organization*

1968 RENÉ CASSIN

1965 *United Nations Children's Fund*

1964 MARTIN LUTHER KING JR.

1963 *International Committee of*

the Red Cross, League of
Red Cross Societies
1962 LINUS PAULING
1961 DAG HAMMARSKJÖLD
1960 ALBERT LUTULI
1959 PHILIP NOEL-BAKER
1958 GEORGES PIRE
1957 LESTER BOWLES PEARSON
1954 *Office of the United Nations High
Commissioner for Refugees*
1953 GEORGE C. MARSHALL
1952 ALBERT SCHWEITZER
1951 LÉON JOUHAUX
1950 RALPH BUNCHE
1949 LORD BOYD ORR
1947 *Friends Service Council,
American Friends Service
Committee*
1946 EMILY GREENE BALCH,
JOHN R. MOTT
1945 CORDELL HULL
1944 *International Committee of
the Red Cross*
1938 *Nansen International Office
for Refugees*
1937 ROBERT CECIL
1936 CARLOS SAAVEDRA LAMAS
1935 CARL VON OSSIETZKY
1934 ARTHUR HENDERSON
1933 SIR NORMAN ANGELL
1931 JANE ADDAMS,
NICHOLAS MURRAY BUTLER
1930 NATHAN SÖDERBLOM
1929 FRANK B. KELLOGG
1927 FERDINAND BUISSON,

LUDWIG QUIDDE
1926 ARISTIDE BRIAND, GUSTAV
STRESEMANN
1925 SIR AUSTEN CHAMBERLAIN,
CHARLES G. DAWES
1922 FRIDTJOF NANSEN
1921 HJALMAR BRANTING,
CHRISTIAN LANGE
1920 LÉON BOURGEOIS
1919 WOODROW WILSON
1917 *International Committee of
the Red Cross*
1913 HENRI LA FONTAINE
1912 ELIHU ROOT
1911 TOBIAS ASSER, ALFRED FRIED
1910 *Permanent International
Peace Bureau*
1909 AUGUSTE BEERNAERT,
PAUL HENRI D'ESTOURNELLES
DE CONSTANT
1908 KLAS PONTUS ARNOLDSON,
FREDRIK BAJER
1907 ERNESTO TEODORO MONETA,
LOUIS RENAULT
1906 THEODORE ROOSEVELT
1905 BERTHA VON SUTTNER
1904 *Institute of International Law*
1903 RANDAL CREMER
1902 ÉLIE DUCOMMUN,
ALBERT GOBAT
1901 HENRY DUNANT,
FRÉDÉRIC PASSY

A Picture Book of
Eleanor Roosevelt

by David A. Adler
illustrated by Robert Casilla

Eleanor Roosevelt was born in New York City on October 11, 1884. Her parents, Anna and Elliot, were wealthy. They had many servants, a home in the city, and a large summer house in the country.

Eleanor's mother was beautiful, but Eleanor was not a pretty child. She was tall and awkward and also very quiet. She often looked so serious that her mother called her "Granny." Eleanor hated that nickname.

Eleanor's father called her his "Little Golden Hair" and his "Little Nell." Eleanor loved those names and she loved her father.

When Eleanor was just eight years old, her mother died. Eleanor went to live in her grandmother's house. Two years later, in 1894, Eleanor's father died, too. Eleanor missed him terribly and dreamed of him often.

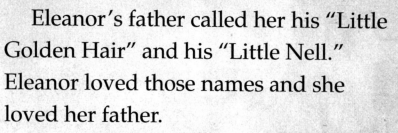

There were many rules in her grandmother's house. Eleanor could not read in bed before breakfast. She had to wear long black stockings and high button shoes even in the summer.

Eleanor was cared for by a servant, Madeleine, who often screamed at her. Sometimes she even pulled Eleanor's hair.

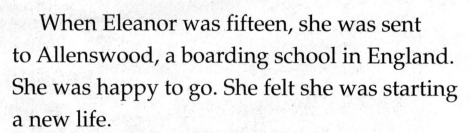

When Eleanor was fifteen, she was sent to Allenswood, a boarding school in England. She was happy to go. She felt she was starting a new life.

The teachers and students at Allenswood thought Eleanor was wonderful. The headmistress wrote home that Eleanor had a pure heart. She taught Eleanor the importance of helping others.

While Eleanor was in England, her uncle, Theodore Roosevelt, became the president of the United States. He was a strong and popular leader.

Eleanor returned to New York in 1902. She was almost eighteen years old.

Eleanor's grandmother sent her from one fancy party to the next. Eleanor usually hated those parties, but she did have a good time when she talked with her distant cousin, Franklin Delano Roosevelt.

Eleanor joined the Junior League and began a lifelong devotion to helping the poor. While working for the Junior League, Eleanor taught children to dance and exercise, in the Rivington Street Settlement House.

Eleanor took her cousin Franklin to the Settlement House. Franklin took her to college football games at his school. They fell in love.

On March 17, 1905, Eleanor and Franklin were married. At the wedding, the guests paid little attention to the bride and groom. They were more interested in Eleanor's uncle, President Theodore Roosevelt.

Eleanor and Franklin had six children—one daughter and five sons. One son died when he was still an infant. Eleanor had servants and nurses to help her. At times, the children were afraid of the strict nurses and so was Eleanor.

Franklin's mother Sara often told Franklin and Eleanor what to do. Sara chose their first house and furniture. During the early years of her marriage, Eleanor didn't complain, but later she refused to be bossed around.

Franklin admired Eleanor's uncle Theodore and
wanted to be just like him. Eleanor helped Franklin
campaign for public office.

In 1921 Franklin was stricken with polio. He couldn't walk after that. When Franklin first became sick, Eleanor was his nurse. Later she went to political meetings and traveled for him. She brought back detailed reports on what she heard and saw.

Franklin was elected governor of New York in 1928 and 1930 and president of the United States in 1932. He was reelected president in 1936, 1940, and 1944. When Franklin became president, Eleanor became first lady.

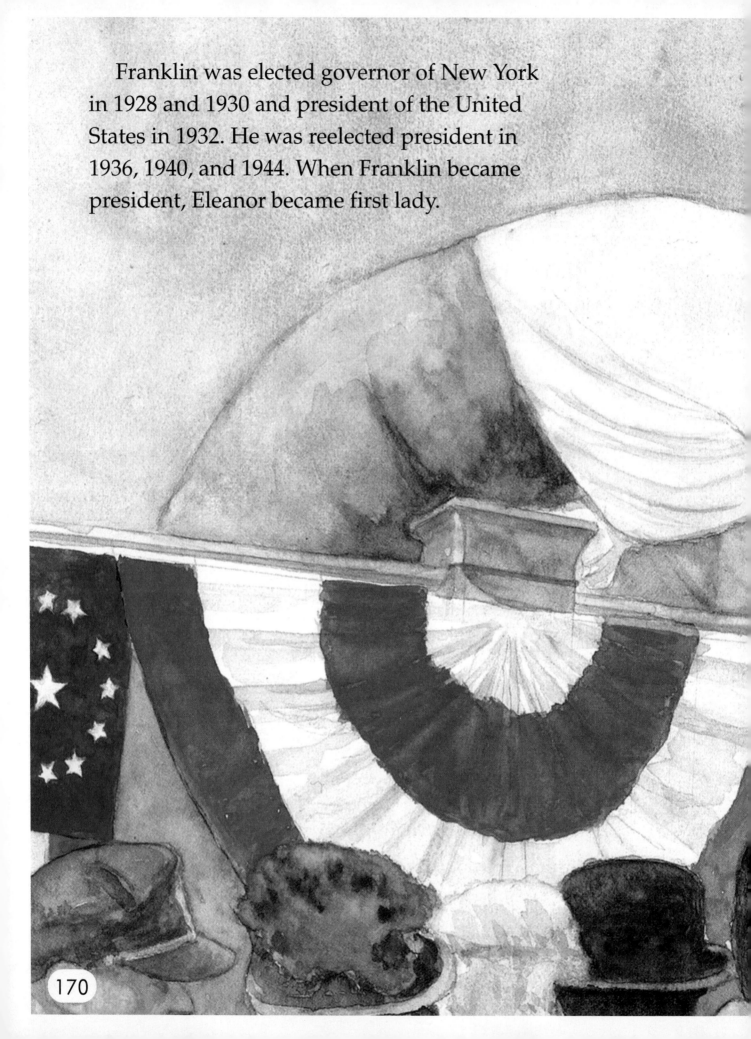

The 1930s was the time of the Great Depression. Banks and factories had closed. Millions of people had lost their jobs. Hungry people stood in long lines for free bread and soup. It was a difficult time to be president or first lady.

Eleanor didn't wait to do things. Her motto was, "Tomorrow is now." She had a radio program and wrote a daily newspaper column. She traveled to cities, towns, farms and into coal mines. She brought hope to millions of people.

Eleanor used the money she earned from her speeches and writings to help the poor.

Eleanor spoke out for women's rights, the rights of the Indians, the homeless, young people, and minorities. She told people, "Do what you feel in your heart to be right." Eleanor always did.

Eleanor belonged to the Daughters of the American Revolution. In 1939 they would not allow a great singer, Marian Anderson, to perform in their hall because she was black. Eleanor quit the group and arranged for Marian Anderson to sing in front of the Lincoln Memorial instead.

On December 7, 1941, the United States' armed forces were attacked at Pearl Harbor, Hawaii. The United States entered the Second World War.

During the war, Eleanor traveled all over the world to visit American soldiers. When she came home, she brought messages from the soldiers to their families.

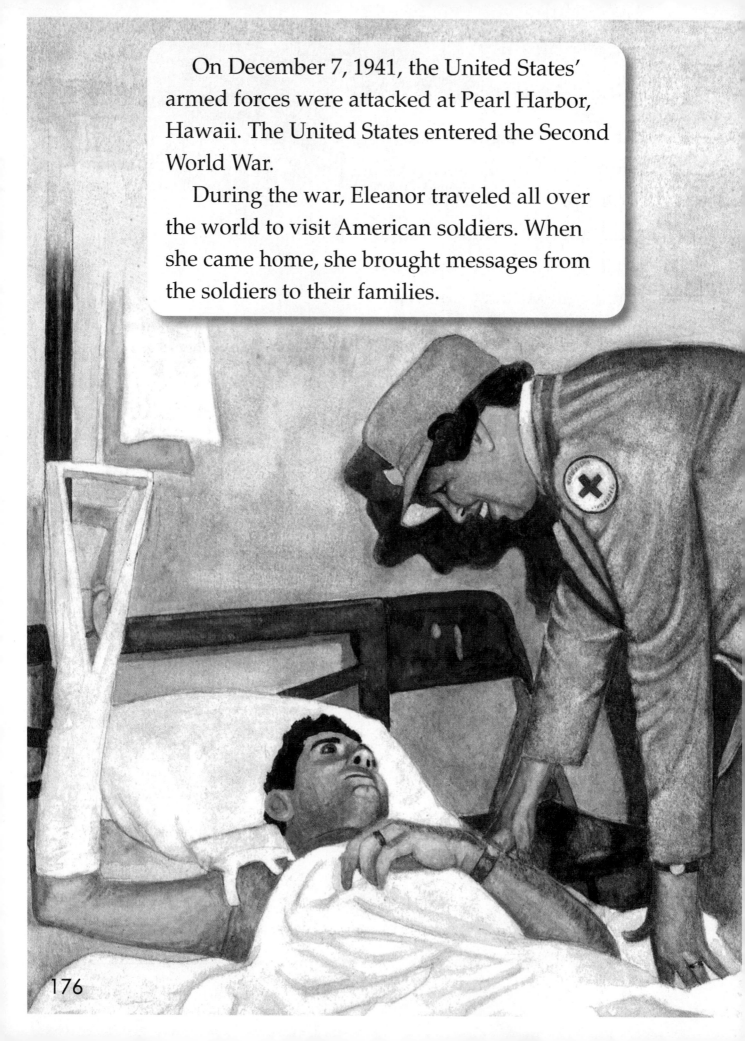

On April 12, 1945, President Franklin Roosevelt died. The whole country mourned with Eleanor.

Eleanor moved out of the White House. She was no longer the first lady, but she did not retire from public life. "Life was meant to be lived," she said.

The war ended a few months later, and Eleanor worked to ensure peace. She was the United States' representative at the new United Nations, where leaders from all over the world could meet and discuss their differences. Eleanor said, "If we are to live together, we have to talk."

While Eleanor was at the United Nations, she was the chairperson of the Commission on Human Rights.

Eleanor was always busy. "You must do the thing you think you cannot do," she said.

Eleanor Roosevelt died on November 7, 1962. She was the most important, most loved woman of her time. President Harry S. Truman called her "First Lady of the World."

IMPORTANT DATES

1884   Born on October 11 in New York City.

1905   Married Franklin Delano Roosevelt on
            March 17.

1921   Franklin was stricken with polio.

1928–1932   Franklin served as governor of New York.

1932–1945   Franklin served as president and Eleanor
            as first lady of the United States.

1945   Franklin died on April 12.

1945–1953   Eleanor served as a delegate to the
            United Nations.

1946–1951   Served as chairperson of the United Nations
            Human Rights Commission.

1962   Died on November 7 at the age of 78.

Every Time I Climb a Tree

by David McCord

Every time I climb a tree
Every time I climb a tree
Every time I climb a tree
I scrape a leg
Or skin a knee
And every time I climb a tree
I find some ants
Or dodge a bee
And get the ants
All over me

And every time I climb a tree
Where have you been?
They say to me
But don't they know that I am free
Every time I climb a tree?
I like it best
To spot a nest
That has an egg
Or maybe three

And then I skin
The other leg
But every time I climb a tree
I see a lot of things to see
Swallows, rooftops and TV
And all the fields and farms there be
Every time I climb a tree
Though climbing may be good for ants
It isn't awfully good for pants
But still it's pretty good for me
Every time I climb a tree

Walk Lightly

by J. Patrick Lewis

Make the Earth your companion.
    Walk lightly on it, as other creatures do.
Let the Sky paint her beauty—she is always
    watching over you.
Learn from the Sea how to face harsh forces.
Let the River remind you that everything will pass.
Let the Lake instruct you in stillness.
Let the Mountains teach you grandeur.
Make the Woodland your house of peace.
Make the Rainforest your house of hope.
Meet the Wetland on twilight ground.
Save some small piece of Grassland for a red kite
    on a windy day.
Watch the Icecaps glisten with crystal majesty.
Hear the Desert whisper hush to eternity.
Let the Town bring you togetherness.
Make the Earth your companion.
    Walk lightly on it, as other creatures do.

Hug O' War

by Shel Silverstein

I will not play at tug o' war.
I'd rather play at hug o' war,
Where everyone hugs
Instead of tugs,
Where everyone giggles
And rolls on the rug,
Where everyone kisses,
And everyone grins,
And everyone cuddles,
And everyone wins.

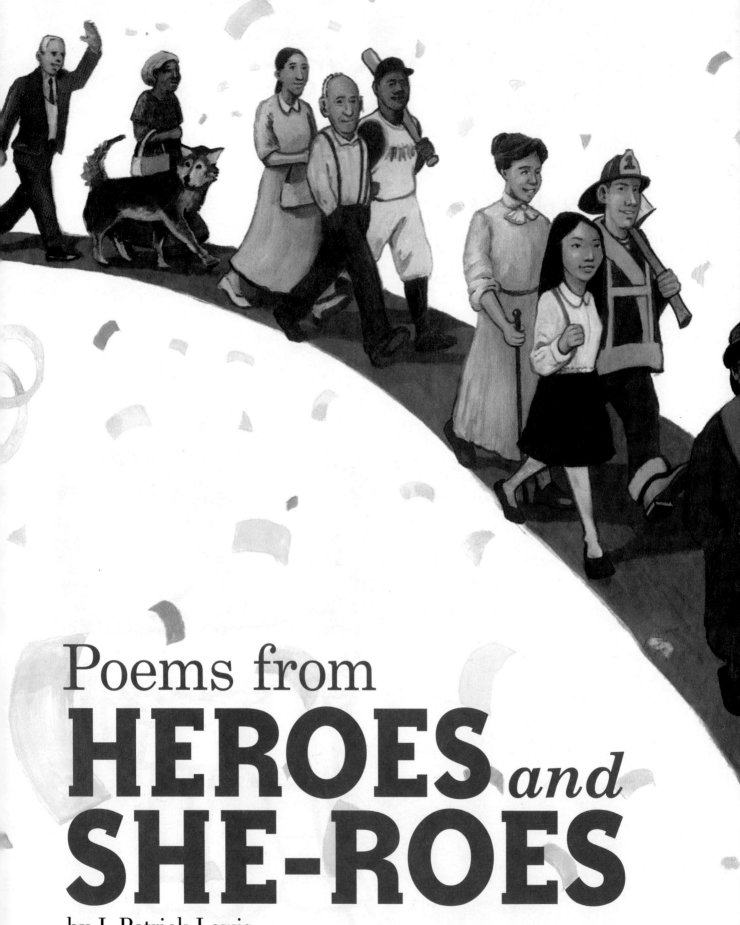

Poems from
HEROES and
SHE-ROES

by J. Patrick Lewis

Give thanks to the he- and she-roes
Who will turn upon a dime
When occasion calls for action—
And be there in half the time.

Roll red carpets out for she-roes
And to heroes raise a toast
For extraordinary courage—
Yet you'll never hear them boast.

Lend your hand to he- and she-roes,
To the valiant and the brave,
To those simple people known by
Two simple words: *They gave.*

So heroes set aside their fear
To lend a hand or lend an ear,

To face the night or save the day
And never look the other way.

They do not, with a single bound,
Leap up tall buildings from the ground.

But from a sense of decency,
They share themselves with you and me.

No matter what or where or who,
When something must be done,
They do.

Text

"Seek the Sun," reprinted by permission of SPIDER Magazine, September 2009, Vol. 16, No. 7, text © 2009 by Phillis Gershator, art © 2009 by Teeun Yoo.

Danger! Earthquakes, by Seymour Simon, used by permission of Star Walk Kids Media. Copyright 2002 by Seymour Simon.

"The Fool on the Hill," from *Tales of Thunder and Lightning* by Harry Devlin. Copyright © 1975. Reprinted by permission of the Devlin Estate.

"Mother of the Mountains," from *Tales of Thunder and Lightning* by Harry Devlin. Copyright © 1975. Reprinted by permission of the Devlin Estate.

"I am BOOM!" from *The Dragons Are Singing Tonight* by Jack Prelutsky, illustrations by Peter Sis. Text copyright © 1993 by Jack Prelutsky, illustrations copyright © 1993 by Peter Sis. Used by permission of HarperCollins Publishers.

"Dragon Smoke," from *I Feel the Same Way* by Lilian Moore. Copyright © 1966, 1967 Lilian Moore. Used by permission of Marian Reiner.

"Who Could Somersault the San Andreas Fault?" from *A World of Wonders: Geographic Travels in Verse and Rhyme* by J. Patrick Lewis, copyright © 2002 by J. Patrick Lewis, text. Used by permission of Dial Books for Young Readers, a division of Penguin Group (USA) LLC.

"Who Could Somersault the San Andreas Fault?" from *A World of Wonders: Geographic Travels in Verse and Rhyme* by J. Patrick Lewis, copyright ©2002 by J. Patrick Lewis. Reprinted by permission of Curtis Brown, Ltd. (USA) LLC.

Johnny Appleseed, by Lola M. Schaefer, excerpted from the work entitled: *Johnny Appleseed* © 2003 by Capstone. All rights reserved.

Going West, by Jean Van Leeuwen, illustrated by Thomas Allen, copyright ©1992 by Jean Van Leeuwen, text, copyright ©1993 by Thomas Allen, illustrations. Used by permission of Dial Books for Young Readers, a division of Penguin Group (USA) LLC.

"Planting a Tree," by Nancy Boyd Turner.

"Trees," from *The Little Hill* by Harry Behn. Copyright 1949 Harry Behn. © renewed 1977 Alice L. Behn. All Rights Renewed and Reserved. Used by permission of Marian Reiner.

"Home on the Range," by Dr. Brewster M. Higley. First published in the December 1873 issue of the *Smith County Pioneer.*

"The Gateway Arch," from *Tour America: A Journey Through Poems and Art* © 2006 by Diane Siebert. Used with permission of Chronicle Books LLC, San Francisco. Visit ChronicleBooks.com

Alfred Nobel: The Man Behind the Peace Prize. Used with permission from Sleeping Bear Press / Cherry Lake Publishing

A Picture Book of Eleanor Roosevelt, text copyright © 1991 by David A. Adler. Illustrations copyright © 1991 by Robert Casilla. A Picture Book of Eleanor Roosevelt. Reprinted by permission of Holiday House, Inc.

"Everytime I Climb a Tree," from *Every Time I Climb a Tree* by David McCord illustrated by Marc Simont. Copyright © 1952 by David McCord. By permission of Little, Brown and Company. All rights reserved.

"Walk Lightly", from A WORLD OF WONDERS: GEOGRAPHIC TRAVELS IN VERSE AND RHYME by J. Patrick Lewis, copyright (c) 2002 by J. Patrick Lewis, text. Used by permission of Dial Books for Young Readers, a division of Penguin Group (USA) LLC. "Walk Lightly" (illustration), from A WORLD OF WONDERS: GEOGRAPHIC TRAVELS IN VERSE AND RHYME by J. Patrick Lewis, illustrated by Alison Jay, copyright (c) 2002 by Alison Jay, illustrations. Used by permission of Dial Books for Young Readers, a division of Penguin Group (USA) LLC.

"Walk Lightly", from A WORLD OF WONDERS: GEOGRAPHIC TRAVELS IN VERSE AND RHYME by J. Patrick Lewis, copyright © 2002 by J. Patrick Lewis. Reprinted by permission of Curtis Brown, Ltd.

"Hug O' War," by Shel Silverstein. Copyright © 1974, renewed 2002 Evil Eye Music, LLC. Reprinted with permission from the Estate of Shel Silverstein and HarperCollins Children's Books.

"Heroes and She-roes," from *Heroes and She-roes: Poems of Amazing and Everyday Heroes* by J. Patrick Lewis, illustrated by Jim Cooke, copyright ©2005 by J. Patrick Lewis, text, copyright ©2005 by Jim Cooke, illustrations. Used by permission of Dial Books for Young Readers, a division of Penguin Group (USA) LLC.

"Heroes and She-roes," from *Heroes and She-roes: Poems of Amazing and Everyday Heroes* by J. Patrick Lewis, copyright © 2005 by J. Patrick Lewis. Reprinted by permission Curtis Brown Ltd, (USA) LLC.

Illustrations

44, 45 Jim Madsen
46 IL Sung Na
184 *Dan Andreasen*

Photographs

Photo locators denoted as follows: Top (T), Center (C), Bottom (B), Left (L), Right (R), Background (Bkgd)

14 David Weintraub/Photo Researchers; **16** Getty Images; **18** National Geophysical Datacenter; **20** J. Dewey/US Geological Survey ; **24** Lloyd Cluff/Corbis; **26** Van Bucher/Photo Researchers; **28** Mehmet Celebi/US Geological Survey ; **30** U.S. Geological Survey; **32** National Geophysical Datacenter; **34** D.Perkins/US Geological Survey ; **36** Garry Gay/Getty Images; **40** Asia File/Alamy; **42** Mehmet Celebi/US Geological Survey ; **52** BrandX Pictures/Bob Rashid/Getty Images; **54** Tom Bean / Alamy; **56** North Wind Picture Archives; **58** Corbis; **60** Carol Cohen/Corbis; **62** Northwind Picture Archives; **64** Bettmann/Corbis; **66** Northwind Picture Archives; **68** Time & Life Pictures/Getty Images; **118** Deni & Will Mcintyre/Getty Images; **119** nadiya_sergey/Shutterstock; **120** Danita Delimont / Alamy; **121**